# I'd Like To Complain
## Getting more than 'sorry'
## when things go wrong

Drew Matthews

Dedicated to my family, who have to put up with the
grumpy phone calls I've made,
and all the call centre staff who's days I may have ruined
by ringing them up.

I'd Like To Complain
Copyright: Drew Matthews
Published: 10<sup>th</sup> June 2013

ISBN-13: 978-1490979953
ISBN-10: 1490979956

# CHAPTER ONE

## *Introduction.*

Nobody likes bad customer service, as a customer you want to feel loved, and feel like you're being treated well, or at least fairly by whatever company you are dealing with.

Although the majority of companies do actually care about their customers, sometimes your 'customer experience' isn't quite the pleasant and wonderful ride it should be, and in todays climate, we need to keep in mind that customers exist to keep companies in business, they aren't just their playthings.

Things go wrong however, thats a fact, we don't live in a perfect world and companies do make genuine mistakes. We have to live with that, but often they are things that could be avoided, and with a little thought on the side of the company you are dealing with, be more palatable for you as one of their customers.

Quite often if something does goes wrong, or you're unhappy with your customer experience, you'll be tempted to write in, send an email, or, maybe ring up and voice your dissatisfaction. The latter is normally the route most take, and having complained to some poor member of staff at the call centre, they will more than often tell you they are sorry, that they will 'take your feedback into consideration,' and that will, in the majority of cases normally be the end of it. If you're lucky, you may get a standard letter from them apologising, and again stressing they have taken on board your comments.

You'll end up having spent money on a phone call, probably got fairly stressed about it, and normally be no better off, mentally or financially.

In this book, I'll explain how to complain effectively, or, if you dislike the word 'complain'; how to make a point, and receive something to make that pain a little better. I'll explain how to get as close to the top of a company as you need to get to obtain the result you want; I'll explain what to do, and how to do it, so that in the majority of cases you'll get something back from the company that broke your customer experience.

But why should you take my advise? Well, I've not only worked in customer service centres, I've also been the one doing the complaining on more than one occasion. People who know me have often asked how I get results, and how I've managed to get the gratuities or good will gestures I have from companies. For over 10 years I've followed a few key points when I've needed to complain to a company. In some of those cases the resulting outcome has been financial, £50 credited to my account, reversal of a charge, a gift voucher, a reduced bill, or obtaining an item for free. In other cases the result has been to fix the issue, and go beyond to provide the service that should have been provided initially. In all cases what I've obtained has made the pain of a company lets say, 'making some mistakes' a little easier to swallow.

I hope the information in this book will be helpful to you, treat it wisely and do not abuse it for personal gain when no wrong has been done. This process will only work when there is a genuine fault on the part of a company against you, it is not a guide to extort freebies from them regardless..

Let us begin…

# CHAPTER TWO

## *What do you want?*

So how do we go about 'complaining'? Where do we start, what do we say when we 'complain'. Personally, I don't like to call it 'complaining' as such, that puts an instant negative feel to the process. I tend to think of this process as more a 'highlighting the errors of their ways'.

This is key to remember throughout the entire process, we are guiding, and highlighting as we go, getting agreements and logically getting rid of anything that allows a company to back out of the fact they messed up, or didn't provide the service you expect from them.

Before we even start talking to the company in question, its best to work out what you want from them as the outcome. You don't have to decide in stone what it is, but you do need to have a general idea. Why? Because otherwise at the critical point where you are asked what you actually want from them, you'll have to think on your feet and come up with something fairly quickly. This isn't a great situation to be in, so just generally get in your mind what would make you a happy customer again, and allow you to overlook whatever mess the company has made of your relationship with them.

Before you start, work out the 'end point' that you want to achieve. It is very important here to be realistic, you're not going to get millions, or a new car from this (although if you do, please keep me in mind)! You're more likely to need to think along the lines of loyalty bonuses, for instance money off your bill every month, a one off ex gratis payment, a small lump sum into your account or by cheque to compensate you without the company admitting fault, or, a reduction in your bill or similar. Whatever that thing is you're looking to obtain, it will be definitely something more than just a 'sorry'.

Now the next thing you need to do before anything else, before picking up the phone and sharing your woe with the company in question, is to make sure that you can call them for free.

You obviously need a number to call to talk to the company, and the first port of call will normally be the companies website, or a quick glance at the bill or communication from them to get that all important 'contact us' number. In the heat of the moment you might just pick up the phone, and call them, but the majority of companies numbers of far from free to call.

Unfortunately, the number given will normally be an 08456, 0870 or similar number, these may look handy but in actual fact they really aren't from the consumer point of view. Why? Well, if you have a package with your telecoms company that includes 'free calls', likelihood is that the 0845 number won't be included in your free calls, and you will end up paying for the privilege of complaining, and normally at a much higher rate than standard 01xx numbers.

If you're ringing from a mobile, and I don't recommend that for one of these calls, you'll find in almost all cases 08xx numbers aren't included in your mobile call package minutes, and will actually cost you considerably more to call. You could, for example, be looking at up to £10 for a 30 minute call to an 0845 number from your mobile. It also gets worse, and in some cases these numbers also give the company you're ringing a cut of the call cost, so you're actually paying the company you're complaining about! The simple answer is you need to ring from a landline, and find a 01xx number, or an 0800 number.

So the first thing to do is to try and find a freephone 0800 number for the company you're trying to ring, or the next best thing, a 01xx number. You'll find that most companies really don't advertise these numbers, the majority provide a 084xx or similar number.

So how do we get these cheaper numbers? There are a few ways, but a great resource for finding these free, or 01xx numbers is the 'Say No to 0870' website which can be found at http://www.saynoto0870.com/. This site provides a way of finding alternative numbers for companies, you can either type in the original 0845, 0870 or similar number and it will list any known non-geographical numbers (these are the 01xx numbers) and freephone (0800) numbers. You can also browse by company and find the numbers that way. I tend to prefer the former method, putting in the companies listed 08456 number. In other cases, you may just need to search the internet to find the cheaper number.

Once you have obtained the phone number you need, you can get ready to make that call. Keep in mind though that this might be along call (expect an initial call to be about 20 to 30 minutes), so make sure that you have this time spare, and you won't need to stop the call half way through. Take a deep breathe, and start dialling...

# CHAPTER THREE
## *Don't make it personal.*

You should never, ever, ever, make a complaint call to a company, personal. What I mean is that you are not complaining (normally) about the person you are talking to, you are complaining about the company itself. Although if your customer service experience from a specific person is so bad (for example they may have been extremely rude) you could be complaining about a person specifically.

However, I have always had most success, and more importantly an easier ride through the system if that complaint is turned around to be a complaint about the company, not the individual.

You'll find that complaining about the person you are talking to isn't going to get you anywhere, firstly it will just alienate you with that person; they are highly unlikely to help you complain about them to their company, no-one is really going to want to help a person who is complaining about them personally. Secondly, your issues are't with this person, this person isn't going to compensate you, or be ultimately responsible for their actions, it's the company itself where the buck will stop.

You need to keep in mind that some staff might assume when you say 'You' that you mean them personally. I've had this experience many times, and it's a common misunderstanding. If you get the idea that they are thinking like this, it is worth pointing out to them what you mean;

*'When I say 'you' I mean your company, company x, not you*

*personally'*

You'll normally be able to tell that they are thinking you mean them, if they start to get defensive and use what I call 'negative I' phrases, for instance things like;

*'I've not spoken to you before so I can't comment'*
*'I'm not saying that you are wrong'*
*'I can't comment on what you have been told previously'*

Many call centre and customer service staff do think that when people are complaining, that they are complaining about them, so its worth distancing your complaints and issues from the person you are talking to. Make sure that your comments are directed towards the company, not the individual. This approach, can sometimes also help your case a little as the customer service staff sometimes feel that they are more detached from the responsibility of whatever has happened to you and more in a situation to help you.

Every little bit of help you can get is worth it, even if that is just passing you up the 'food chain' to a higher authority than who you are currently talking to.

During your call, I would advise you to, for the majority of the time, stand up. This may sound quite odd, but standing up will make you come across in your voice as more confident and more assertive. It will also help you sound more factual and correct. Sitting down means that you will normally be more relaxed, and you will find that it will come across in your voice and the way you speak during your call.

You can also mix standing up and sitting down, I will normally stand up whilst stating any facts, and during any negotiations or requests. However I will sit down when I want the member of staff to empathise with me, or I want to sound more 'soft' and approachable. If the call isn't going quite according to plan, you can also use the sitting down approach to slow the conversation down, relax it, and try and steer it back on track.

# CHAPTER FOUR

## *Working up the food chain.*

When you contact a company, you will normally start at the lowest customer facing person in the company, no offence to them, many do a wonderful job, but they will be the initial point of contact with a customer. They will get calls similar to yours, day in, day out. They normally don't have a huge amount of decision making power or authority, and normally won't be able to provide a whole host of solutions to your problems (at least not the solutions we might be looking for here).

You can sometimes get lucky and get an outstanding member of staff who solves your problem within that single call. It has happened, and I'm always delightfully pleased when that actually happens. However, in reality, you will need to move onto other people to get the result that you're looking for. I call this 'moving up the food chain' and I'll refer to this numerous times within this book, I will also talk about 'foot holes' which are other ways that you can climb up the 'food chain' to reach the end result that you want. I will give some examples of 'foot holes' later on, but they are very important in allowing you to move up to another person, or, put pressure onto a company to agree with you.

One of the key things to success in this process is being able to move up within the company to talk to someone at a higher level who can provide you the solution you want; There is no point in just moving from person to person unless you are talking to a new person who has more power, and a better ability to resolve your issue. The key thing here is to find someone higher in 'the food chain' who can make you a 'happy, loyal customer' again. I'd never refer to the phrase 'moving up the food chain' when talking to a company, but I will quite often refer to the latter; 'making me a happy, loyal customer.' It is also very important to get agreement through a 'yes' or 'no' answer, and we'll talk about that later on as well.

As I have said, many first line call centre supervisors can actually solve your issues, but in the majority of cases, depending on what you want the outcome to be, you're likely to need to move up the 'food chain' to get the result you want, how high depends on what your goal is, and how serious you feel the problem is. This is the thing that can take time, remember at the start I said these calls could take a long time.

Keep in mind that absolutely *nobody* in the 'food chain' of a company is inaccessible to you.

You, as a customer *can* get right up to the Chief Executive Officer (CEO), believe in that, ignore the 'I'm sorry you cannot talk to them' and you'll be fine.


It's a common misunderstanding that the first person you talk to when you phone a call centre is the person you will continue to talk to. This is definitely not the case, in pretty much all cases you will have to talk to at least 2 people, maybe more to get to the answer and resolution that you want. The single most important person is 'Your manager'.

This is basically the person 'above' this person in that all important food chain. If you are not getting the answer you want from the person you are talking to, politely ask to 'talk to their manager'.

You are likely at this point to get a number of answers, normally none of these are 'ok, please wait whilst I transfer you. You are more likely to get answers such as;
*"I can get a manager to call you back"*
*"I'm sorry there are no managers available"*
*"I cant transfer you"*
*"Can I help?"*
Call backs are horrible things;
*'Calling me back at your connivence as opposed to mine isn't a*

*great customer experience, I have an issue, I'd like it dealt with now please...'*

Normally knocks the suggestion of a call back out, you can also (if you are dealing with a bank or other financial organisation) state that in all likelihood when they do ring you, they will ask you security questions to confirm your identify. Most companies advise you not to give out personal and security information to unknown callers. Let them know clearly that you would rather not confirm security questions to an unknown caller, and again, ask to talk to a manager, and move up the food chain.

Whatever the answer, you, as a customer have the right to talk to a manager. If the first request to talk to a manager falls on deaf ears, ask again, politely!;

*'Can I talk to your manager'*

You may this time get very informative (if not wholly unhelpful) answers such as;

*"They will tell you the same as me"*

*"They will need to ring you back"*

*"I cant transfer you"*

Again, you have to stick to your guns and ask again, at this point you should also remind them of the fact you've asked already;

*"I have now asked you twice to talk to a manager, and twice you have ignored that request, will you please now transfer me to a manager".*

Repeat your request exactly the same as previously;

*'Can I talk to your manager'.*

It may take some time to actually get through to a manager, but in 90% of cases this repeated process will get you to talk to the next up the food chain (the most I've ever had to ask is 7 times)!

When you do get through to the manager, again politely explain the number of times that you've had to ask to talk to them, make sure that they are aware that their staff seemed to want to stop you talking to the manager (they may not be aware of this);

*"I've had to ask repeatedly x times to be transferred to a manager, I don't expect to have to repeatedly ask to have my call escalated..."*

Now is the time to again confirm who you are talking to,

although many managers will introduce themselves;

*"Hello Mr Matthews, I'm Darren the call centre manager,"* try and get a call centre ID for that manager, or at the least a full name. Remember that staff are required to give you their call centre ID's even if they won't provide their names, a failure to do that, is a whole complaint in itself (especially if the company is a bank)!

A classic line that will quite often come up here from the manager is;

*"What appears to be the problem.."* Or *"How can I help?"*

You can immediately knock them onto their back foot by asking if their colleague explained the issue to them, or just passed them across blindly. In most cases, staff are responsible enough to explain at least their view on the issue, but it's not always the case. From a customer service point of view, the manager should have most of the facts, but, you need to face the fact that during this process you will have to explain yourself many, many, many times, and probably a few more, just to be sure.

Its also worth confirming that the person you are talking to is actually a manager, it has been known for call centre staff to just pass you across to another, if they have, get that call centre ID and store it away for later use when you do find a manager.

# CHAPTER FIVE

*Don't be rude, be factual and bluff.*

There are some very, very important things you should keep in mind when talking to members of staff with the company. One of those things is worth highlighting on it's own, it's the golden rule:

You should never, ever be rude, shout, or be abusive to any member of a call centre or company staff.

Even if this company has been truly appalling in their treatment of you, being rude, shouting, or being abusive is absolutely the worse thing you can do; call centre staff are quite within their rights to 'terminate' the call under these circumstances, especially if you are in any way abusive or threatening towards them, again keep in mind what I mentioned earlier about not getting personal, talk about the company, not the individual.

Keep in mind that in the same way that you should be polite and not rude to the call centre staff, they also *should* behave the same way to you. For instance, it's not ok for them to just terminate a call because they are bored of you, or don't know how to deal with you. It's not acceptable for them to just put you on hold and pass you onto another person without at least asking you if they can, or even telling you thats what they are going to do. If they do any of these things, these are classed as 'foot holes', a reason to stop talking to this person and move up 'the food chain'

Don't ever swear (even if you find it acceptable to swear in your normal day to day life), don't even consider using words that you personally might not consider offensive;

Don't use the words 'pissed off,' 'crap' or 'shit' however tempting it is to do so. Make sure you always use politically correct and inoffensive phrases;

*'I'm extremely unhappy..'*
*'Totally inadequate..'*
*'Lost all confidence in..'*
*'Totally unacceptable..'*

Having a call terminated or disconnected for being offensive will drop you back down the food chain very quickly, and also put you in a bad position for continuing your dialogue with the company. Think of it a little like a game of 'snakes and ladders', we want to move up quickly, and avoid sliding down!

You must be at all times factual, and polite. It is also best if you don't physically get upset or angry (even if you feel like doing so)!, focus on the facts, focus on whats been done incorrectly, and focus on the effect, and by all means make the company feel guilty.

Throughout this entire process of talking with a company, you will, and I'll make no secret of this, have you bluff your way through it quite a bit.

Bluffing, is very different to lying. I'd not recommend at all to lie about anything during your conversation about your complaint. Firstly, you'll get found out very easily, and normally quite quickly, and secondly you'll also need to remember your lies, and you really don't want any more work in this process. Stick to the facts, but you will need to bluff.

Bluffing in this case is just making sure that you appear, or sound as if you know what you're on about, and most importantly, that you know your rights and position better than the company you're complaining to, whilst, still keeping credible! You may also talk about things that you may do, or be able to do, for example, my next call will be to your CEO.

You'll be surprised just how easy this is; if you sound, and appear to be very confident about facts and the way things should be working, you're much more likely to move along quicker to a suitable solution to your problem. Few call centre staff, be they first line staff, supervisors or managers will check or disagree with what you are saying if you sound confident enough about it. Just make sure you're not coming up with completely unbelievable things.

When dealing with companies either in person, or through their call centres and customer service centres, I prefer facts rather than guess work, and I don't like people making assumptions.

It's a simple fact that I could sit at home and guess at what they might say without ringing them; I can also imagine what they might say without ringing them, and I can probably assume the outcome, all without ringing or contacting them in any way whatsoever. This isn't what I want to do, I'd rather a discussion with a company where things aren't assumed or guessed at, and they are confident in their responses.

The simple fact is that when I contact a company to make a complaint, I do it because I want an outcome, I want facts, and I want explanations and solutions. I don't want guesswork or wishy washy answers and explanations, and I urge you to also ask them for the same.

If you are getting responses to your questions, or explanations from them that use words like;

*'I think...'*

*'Maybe..'*

*'Probably..'*

*'Possibly..'*

*'Almost certainly..'*

Then you'll need to steer the service advisor back onto a factual track by stating to them;

*'There are a lot of maybes, possibly's, I think and probably's in there.. Which sounds like you're not really sure'*

They might say that those uncertain words are just a turn of phrase, which they probably are, however, lets take an example;

*'My manager should be available in probably about 15 minutes'*

Which if you think about it, actually is saying that my manager *might* be available, they *might* be available in 15 minutes, but to be honest, I don't know. This doesn't instil confidence that *anyone*, let alone a manager will ring you back.

Here I would politely explain that you'd like factual responses, if they don't know, then please pass me to someone that does know these answers for certain. This allows you to move up the food chain. If they don't know the answer (by using mights, probably, maybe's), this is a foot hole, move on;

What you are doing here is moving 'up the food chain,' normally you can request to move onto their manager, who will, normally have more power and decision making abilities that this person. This is one of the easiest and simplest 'foot holes' there are.

# CHAPTER SIX

## *Foot Holes and Language.*

So, what is a foot hole? Put simply, a foot hole is a way to climb up the food chain to someone who will resolve your problem for you, and give you the outcome that you want from your complaint.

*Physically* what they are is a little bit more complex to explain, however, lets look at them in a bit more detail, as they are one of the major things you have in your arsenal.

A foot hole could be a slip up on the facts that the company tell you that contradict themselves, meaning that maybe the company isn't telling you the truth, or they just haven't checked and are trying to fob you off.

It could also be just down to the way that you're treated by the company, or the way they address you.

A foot hole could be the number of times something specifically has happened to you, or it could be something you're being told by the company that logically, just doesn't make sense.

A foot hole could be someone not being available. For instance, if you ask to talk to a manager, and you're told that they aren't available, but they will call you back, ask to talk to that managers manager.

A foot hole may be you loosing confidence in the person you're talking to by the language they are using, things like maybe's, probably's, might's and other words that aren't factual.

Basically, a foot hole is something that helps you stop the conversation, and move onto getting closer to your 'end point'. A foot hole is in essence a 'Look that isn't right' moment which can be used as leverage to either progress you further to a resolution, or to move onto a higher person in the food chain.

Depending on the 'foot hole' you have, you might abandon your original complaint and pursue this one instead to achieve some sort of resolution.

One such, although extreme case, was when a call centre member of staff called the customer 'stupid,' which probably breaks all the basic rules of providing good customer service to your customer, this could immediately be used as a foot hole to move onto a much more senior member of staff to discuss this problem.

In the same way that you don't expect wishy washy answers and words from the person you're talking to, you should try and do the same back. The words you use when you talk to staff can change a question or request into an instruction, or at the very least come across as more confident, to allow a further instruction later on.

*'I think you have made an error with my bill.'*

Isn't very positive, it provides an 'out' for the company to say that they haven't, its doubtful, and doubtful means that it's not set in stone and is open to being dismissed.

*'You have made an error with my bill this month.'*

Is factual, confident, and isn't a request or something that is assumed. It is a set in stone fact from your point of view. Its much harder for a customer service adviser to disagree with the statement without sounding like they are completely knocking you down.

You can also use words to drive the conversation down a route that can only result in a 'Yes' answer or action. A 'No' or negative response can kill the conversation or request dead, which will leave you stuck with nowhere to go. In all conversations, you need to make sure that you don't provide a route to a 'no' or negative response.

*'Can you please put £25 into my account as a sign of goodwill?'*

Can be responded to as yes, or no, it's a question. If it's a 'no, we can't do that' you can't really beg them, or ask again. The request is basically dead in the water. Your route here is then going nowhere.

17

*'I have spent 30 minutes on the phone with you, you have now resolved my issue, a gesture of goodwill on your part will help resolve this fully'*

This is not a 'yes or no' statement, you need to steer the conversation down the route towards what it is your desire to make you a happy customer again. You also aren't closing the conversation here. You aren't saying '*a gesture of goodwill on your part will resolve this fully,*' you're saying that it will help, allowing you to continue should you still feel that something else needs to be done to address the situation.

Using words or phrases like 'you need to..,' And not 'I think, Maybe, Possibly' etc. will put you in a more commanding position.

# CHAPTER SEVEN

## *Establishing a Yes or No Answer.*

I find many call centre staff to be very noncommittal about agreeing, or for that matter, disagreeing with anything you say.

They tend to take the line of what I call neutral answers, they neither say yes or no, to any statement that you make about the service they have provided.

For instance, questions to them such as; *'Would you be happy if you had received the same treatment from a company?'* would be met with a very noncommittal *'I can't comment on that'* or *'I can't say'*. Questions that even hint to suggesting that they company might not be that great, are even harder to get a straight answer on; *'Do you feel that company x has provided a good service to me?'* are most likely to get a very fuzzy answer.

The trick is to get a firm 'Yes' or 'No' as your answer, normally things like has the company treated you well? Once you can get a firm 'No' or 'Yes' to question or a fact, you can set it in stone. For instance, if you can get agreement, basically getting a 'Yes' to a question, you can hold that fact in favour of your case, they are (as a representative of company x) confirming a fact or statement you have made;

*'I haven't been fairly treated by you have I?'*

*'You lost the parcel I paid you to deliver, didn't you?'*

*'You exposed my personal details to a third party without my permission didn't you?'*

You must phrase all these questions in a way that the only real answer is either yes, or no. You will normally get a noncommittal answer, so you need to repeat the question and then add; 'Yes or No?';

*'I haven't been fairly treated by you have I? Yes, or No?'*

You may yet again get something other than yes.. Or no... in which case you need to clearly state that they aren't answering the question and this is a simple yes, or no answer.

If they refuse to commit to yes or no, then again use it as a 'foot hole' and move up the food chain, ask to be transferred to their manager, or supervisor.

If the answer comes back as the reverse of what you'd like; *'I haven't been treated fairly have I?'* — *'yes you have'* then you will need to 'reframe' that back to the staff member to demonstrate how thats isn't a great answer;

*'I haven't been treated fairly have I?'*

*'Yes, you have.'*

*'So it's company x's policy to display customer service to their customer by .....'*

Again you are phrasing this statement/question into a 'Yes..' or 'No..' Focusing once again on getting that yes or no and not any other type of answer.

No company is actually going to say it's their policy to treat customers badly, but they are also not going to say, normally, that whatever they have done in your case is normal policy. What we are trying to do here is to establish a yes no answer again. If it's not the companies policy to treat customers badly, and, lets be honest, no companies policy is going to be that, it must, by logic mean that you've not be treated in line with their policy of dealing with customers.

Its very useful sometimes to put the call centre staff into your situation, at least to again try and get some 'agreement' answers.

One way of doing this is to use an example of your situation with the staff, explain something similar and ask them how they would feel. This is the only time when you should be talking at a personal level, as opposed to talking about the company.

Lets take an example of say a company repeatedly doing the same thing wrong, and repeatedly saying 'sorry';

*"So, let say for instance I ran over your cat, and said sorry, you*

*might accept that. If I ran over your cat again the following day, and said sorry, and then did it again the next day, and the day after. Would you feel that sorry, wasn't quite the word to use?'*

Again here we are looking for a 'Yes' or 'No' answer. You may again get an answer that isn't a yes or no, they may say that for example running over a cat isn't relevant, stick to your guns, be stubborn, you are trying to prove a point, keep at it until they provide a 'Yes' or 'No'. Demonstrate to them the pain you've gone through.

# CHAPTER EIGHT

## *Little known facts.*

Sometimes your call might be quite short, and you may only have to talk with a single person. A little known fact is that almost all call centre staff (although they won't tell you this), can provide some sort of monetary compensation, although it might not be a huge amount, you can quite easily get up to £25 payment from a single call to a single person.

Most call centre staff will say that they need to calculate, or authorise with their manager, but the bottom line is that they can provide a compensation fee to you, without to much hassle. For example if the phone number is normally an 0845 number, and you'd been on the phone for 20 minutes, a reasonable 'gesture of goodwill' to cover the call would be around £20. Although in practise you will have followed the advice at the start of this book, and found an 0800 number, or 01xx number, so, in fact you have not paid anything for the call.

Call centre ID's are wonderful things, if not always known about by everyone, including the call centre staff themselves! Normally, call centre staff will only provide you their first name, this is normally for their privacy or personal security, although quite why you are polite enough to provide them with both your first and second name, but they cannot, is another matter.

Its pretty unlikely if you ring the company again and ask to talk to 'Maggie' that you are going to get through to the same person you spoke to previously. A 'call centre id' or 'operator id' is a way that an employee within the call centre can be identified without using any of their personal details.

Call centre staff should know their call centre id's, although they might know them as something else, so you might need to explain a little as to what you're looking for. They are required to know that ID, and if asked by a customer they are required to give it (or if they are not prepared to do that, give their full name and centre location). If they don't provide it, either by refusing, or by not knowing it, you can strike another big black mark in your arsenal, and a 'foot hole' to move up the 'food chain'.

If the conversation isn't going the way you wish, ask the operator for their call centre ID. If the staff member refuses to give you, or doesn't know their ID, ask again, and state what you've done;

*"I've now asked you politely x times for your call centre ID, and you have refused to provide it, you are aware that you are required to provide it if a customer asks for it?"*

You'll need to follow the route up the food chain after this, either armed with, or without their call centre ID. If you don't have it, and you manage to get through to a manager, reiterate the repeated requests for the call centre ID and the failure to provide it, if you get through and you do have the ID, provide it to the manager;

*"I have spoken with your colleague, Maggie, her call centre ID was 1234"*

In many call centres all calls are recorded, if there is a playback of a call, you're providing the trail of people in this call, again, being polite, and following what I've mentioned earlier will mean the call sounds, on your side, polite, controlled and factual. In all cases, follow what I have said previously about how to talk, the language to use, how to move on with 'foot holes', and your side of the call will sound sensible, logical, and hard to argue with.

# CHAPTER NINE

## *Not knowing their own business.*

The thing that really bugs me the most about talking to companies is when they say; '*I don't know*' when it's a simple fact that they should know. Admittedly there isn't anyone in the world that knows everything, the phrase '*I don't know*' should always be followed by a route to find that answer out, for example, '*I don't know, but let me transfer you to...*'

Talking to a member of staff that uses the phrase '*I don't know*' or '*I'm not sure*' normally means they aren't the right person for you, and you need to move up the food chain. Again, this is a foot hole; The simple answer that normally moves me on is the following nine words:

'*Then can I talk to a person who does..*'

Again this puts the company representative into a situation where they can either say 'Yes' and move you up the food chain, normally to their manager; but make sure you're not being transferred onto another random person, or they say 'No,' which if you think about it isn't a very customer service friendly way of replying; '*Can I....*' - '*No*'

You also want to keep this, as always, polite. If they reply with 'No' remind them that you have just asked for something and they have flatly refused to fulfil that quite simple request, ask again to be transferred to someone who does know the answer, normally, they will move you on here, but again if they don't, point out what they are doing, and politely point out that you'd really like an answer to your question or request, and as they have said they don't know the answer, you'd like to talk to someone who can answer it. Again, be stubborn, repeat your request until it's fulfilled.

Quite often you'll find you're popped on hold whilst your call centre staff member talks to 'their manager' or 'their supervisor' or 'a colleague'. This gives you a perfect opportunity to leap up the food chain, but there is a way to play this one.

If you ask a question and your staff member 'checks with someone' thats ok, nobody knows everything. But if you ask something and they again 'double check' with someone, now is the time to ask to talk to that person directly. Again the staff member might try and keep you, but a simple, and polite, '*I just thought it might be easier for me to talk directly to the person you're asking*' should move you on.

They may still try and stop you moving on, common responses here that I've heard are things like;

'*They are on another call at the moment..*'

So how can they answer and talk to you then?

'*I can't transfer calls*'

Rubbish, a call centre that cannot move calls to a supervisor really shouldn't be a call centre

'*They don't talk to customers*'

Er, really?

In all cases, if your call centre person is asking someone else the answer to your questions… move on.. Talk to that person, not this one, move up the food chain with this as a foot hole.

You expect a painter and decorator to be able to paint and decorate, you expect a plumber to be able to plumb, and you expect a parcel delivery company to, well, deliver parcels, right?

Well, yes, but as you've probably found out not all companies actually manage to do what you want them to do, or even do what they specifically imply they do. As mentioned elsewhere in this book, the confirmation by the company of a statement by you, is very important. Getting a 'yes' or an agreement to a statement or question by the company, is drawing a line and setting in stone that it is correct.

"*Are you a bank?*"

The answer, for a bank, should, obviously be 'yes', yet if they have failed to behave like a bank, tell them.

"*Then why have behaved in a way that seems to imply that you are not?*"

This is a no get out answer for them. However they answer, they are either telling you they have failed you (by not behaving like a bank), or they are not a bank (which is an unlikely answer). If they seem not to want to answer a question like this, hit the severity of the failure home to them;

"*If you aren't able to behave like a bank, thats fine, you just need to tell me you're not a bank*".

Again the response to this will never be a bank (or whatever type of company you are talking to) saying that they are not a bank. You are setting in stone here that they *are* a bank (or whatever) and should behave like one.

# CHAPTER TEN
## *Callbacks and statistics.*

When asking to talk to a manager or supervisor, you will quite often be told that they can arrange a 'call back' from the manager or supervisor. This might seem quite handy, however, lets look at what's wrong with 'arranging a call back';

You took the time to ring the company to try and resolve your issues with them. In response, they are saying that they can't deal with it at the moment, and they will contact you when it's convenient for them to discuss it.

It's not a great customer experience, you'll need to sit, wait, and at some point, hopefully expect a call from someone at the company to discuss the problem. However, you might be working when they ring, you might be otherwise engaged, you might be out and about. Taking a call back like this immediately puts you on a back foot. You might not be prepared to take the call, you may not have prepared what you want to say to them. This all means that the company calling is holding the upper ground as they are talking with you at their convenience, not yours.

The other big issue with a 'call back' is security. If you are dealing with anything that involves your account, money, or general identity, they will want to confirm you are, who you say you are. They will expect you to pass through security checks to make sure they are talking to you, and not someone who is just pretending to be you. Although statistically it would be not be very likely you'd get a call from someone phishing your personal details to commit fraud after you've called into a company to complain, but it is possible. I've explained this many times to companies who have rung me directly and asked to confirm security details with me, they really never seem to understand the issue. What if I'm out in public? Do I want to tell them my mothers maiden name, with who knows who is listening? Do I even want to discuss any of my personal identify information in public? If we don't want to do that, and we say that we'll ring them back when it's convenient, then we start the whole process again, and effectively you are back to stage one.

Another major issue with 'call backs' except for the lack of customer service and the potential security issues, is the time. Call backs are normally scheduled to take place within 24 hours, some companies I have spoken to have even quoted up to 48 hours to call you back. This means that at any point within the next 2 days, customer services will ring you back, and normally ask you 'what the problem is..'. Call backs mean that you're placed on the back boiler and are then waiting on the company to contact you.

I'd much rather be in the driving seat when talking with company and always refuse call backs unless I'm at the chief executive level or similar. The question is; how do you refuse a call back? How do you turn the situation around so that you are actually transferred onto the person that would have done the call back anyhow?

The answer is very simple; Keep asking to be transferred.

Be careful what they say after you ask though. They may try and move you into giving a negative response by saying something like;

'Are you refusing to take a call back to deal with your complaint'

'I'm unable to deal with your complaint unless your take a call back'

Whatever they say, always respond in the following phrasing;

'I want this resolved, but a call back is not acceptable. I'm on the phone now, we are discussing the problem, and if you feel you cannot deal with the complaint, pass me onto your manager, or escalations to deal with it'

Again you might be thrown a curve ball, with a response again that says its impossible to pass you through to any other department, and a call back is the only possible option.

I guarantee that if you ask politely, firmly and repeatedly, you will get though to the next person in the food chain.

I'm not great at maths, if I'm talking with a company I dislike when 'statistics' get bounced around;

'In 99.9% of cases…'

'Almost all of our customers'

'Its very rare..'

In 99% (pun totally intended) of cases, they aren't real statistics, and will just be comments that member of staff will make. Quite often these 'statistics' will totally contradict what you are told elsewhere, even sometimes on the same call, with the same person. One of my all time favourites was with a parcel delivery company;

'*We have very few cases of parcels not being returned to senders…*'

And later in the call with the same person;

'*..because of the high volume of parcels at our returns centre we cannot check every single one*'

Both of these statements cannot be turn, however it is 100% true that I heard these exact words, from the same person on the same conversation on the phone!

So how do you deal with 'statistics' being the stopping point on your conversation? Simple, ask.

'*Is that an official statistic?*'

Will probably get a 'err… no' in which case you can politely point out that really they shouldn't make up facts on the fly just to try and make an excuse, or to make out that there isn't a problem with customer service.

This is a fairly strong foot hole; you cannot trust the information being provided by this representative, so you'd like to talk to their manager or escalations; allowing you further up the food chain.

Also point out just how pointless the number they might have given you is; You'll probably find that the most common statistic given is the wonderful 99.9%, making you the 0.1%. If this is a repeated problem with the company from your point of view, then 0.1% most likely isn't a very representative number;

'*I've had an issue the last three times I've ordered, meaning that in my case in the last three orders with you, in 100% of cases for me, its gone wrong.*'

# CHAPTER ELEVEN

## *If you don't like the answer.*

One very important thing to remember is that the answer, whatever that answer is, isn't always the answer you have to accept. If the answer isn't one that you like, don't accept it. Work on them until you get an answer that you do like.

It's very common for people just to accept whatever comes back from a company in regard to their complaint. However, you will find that whatever you are prepared to accept, is exactly what you will get.

This doesn't mean that you have to reject every answer that comes back to you, far from it. If the answer makes sense and you are happy with it, and this is the most important part; it logically makes sense and is reasonable, then its probably best to go with that answer.

However, if you feel that you are being fobbed off, or mislead, or as in most cases where an answer isn't satisfactory, or the answer is contradicting something else you have been told, then its best to reject that answer and ask the company for another solution or answer, again, this is a foot hole; move onto a manager, escalations, or further up the food chain, to obtain the answer that you feel will resolve your issue for you.

So how do you actually get another answer from the company that you're talking to?

The simplest way to just to say;

'*I'm sorry that answer isn't acceptable*'

That can sound very much like a stop statement, in that there isn't a 'yes' or positive move from that statement. In many cases you may just get silence, or more often, you may get a repeat of the same answer.

Again, repeat the same statement again, but ask to move on from this person;

*'I'm sorry that isn't an acceptable answer, can you transfer me to your manager?'*

Continue that process until you move on.

# CHAPTER TWELVE

## *Getting attention.*

Years ago, if you had a problem with a company, your voice to complain publicly about that was fairly small. In todays connected world, the internet has become a powerful resource, it gives everyone a voice, with news spreading like wild fire, as does customer dissatisfaction.

Consumers use the internet to decide what to buy, who to use for their services, and decide who's good, and who to avoid. You may use twitter, you may use Facbook, you may have a blog, or a website, all these (especially high traffic systems such as Twitter and Facbook) can reach a huge number of people, very quickly. This is evident now from the number of companies who have dedicated Twitter or Facbook accounts handling consumer comments or feeling about their company.

Check these accounts, see whats happening, see if other customer have experienced the same as you. If you're told whatever the problem is you're having isn't typical, point them to the public information that indicates it is typical.

If you don't get the answers you need, remind the company of the power of the public voice, say that you are quite happy to document the experience and information that you've been given during your complaint on the internet. However, if you want to play this card, don't do it in a threatening way. Just point out how quickly that information can become public, replied to, and passed on.

I recently discovered a department within a company called

'Brand Damage Limitation' purely by stating the above, the mention that I was going to publicly document my experience, seemed to ring alarm bells, and I was instantly transferred to this department. They quickly resolved the issue, provided a discounted package (totalling a saving of about £370 a year), additional hardware (approximately £120), and additional connectivity (about £37) as way of a 'recompense'. Meaning, yes, I was a happy customer again, the company had no brand damage, and everything carried on normally again.

This might sound slightly odd, but sometimes to get the company to see your side, you do need to point out to a company what they have done, and what they are going to do about it. This approach is basically a "*I want you to think about what you've done, and let me know when your sorry and want to make it better*" conversation. Much like you'd explain to a small child about being naughty, but, its important to try, as best you can, not to sound condescending or patronising here. Normally you use this kind of approach when they ask you '*what do you want me to do?*', you should reply with something clear and simple, for example;

"*I want you to consider what you've done, how it makes me feel as a customer, and what you think you need to do to make me a happy and loyal customer again*".

You can normally finish your call here as it's a very powerful way of putting the onus on them. It puts them in the position of if they do nothing, is it effectively saying that you're not a valued customer, or worse they don't want you as a customer. If they don't do anything then obviously you can use this as a 'foot hole'; as they have done nothing to fix the situation, you are clearly, to them, not very important.

# CHAPTER THIRTEEN

## *How to Leave, even if you don't intend to.*

One of your strongest weapons in your arsenal is leaving whatever provider you are with and going to someone else. Or, in fact the strongest weapon you have in your arsenal is making them think you are about to leave. You should use the notion of leaving as a last resort, or, to gain a major jump up the food chain.

But, we might not actually want leave this company and go to another provider. This company, even if we are complaining about them, might be the actual company we want to be with!

This means that there is a fair amount of bluffing you will need to do at this point, unless of course your goal is to leave! Remember one of the first things we did; 'What are we trying to do here?' - establishing what we actually want to get out of this.

Assuming you don't actually want to terminate your contract or arrangement with the company, discussing leaving normally moves the solution on a little quicker. In todays market, companies should, although they don't always, be falling over themselves to keep you as a customer.

Think about the outcome; you will spend the money for, say a digital TV subscription, the company will get your money. If however, you leave the company you're currently with, then they will get none of your money, and likelihood is that their competitor will. Its as simple as saying; "*Would you like 100% of my money, or, nothing*".

The magic word that you need as a consumer, is 'retentions'. This little word can work miracles sometimes!

There are departments, although well hidden, in all companies that are tasked solely with keeping customers from leaving. These people can be extremely useful to you, as their sole purpose in life is to make sure you stay as a customer, no matter what is needed.

'Retentions' tend to be able to magically come up with better deals to keep you happy than normal call centre staff, these people are tasked with or even rewarded for keeping customers. You will of course normally get a better outcome from them if you are a longer term customer, but in all cases the process of finding and taking on a new customer actually costs a company money. They should, if they are thinking logically, want to save that money. Keeping you is a lot cheaper than trying to get another customer to replace you. If they don't see that, you are well advised to point it out to them at this point.

A good example of this working is when you have exhausted discussions with normal call centre staff and you're not getting what you desire from them. At this point you should stop the conversation, and simply ask to talk to retentions. The wording is, I think quite important, don't say;

*"I'd like to leave then"*

Use the wording;

*"I'd like to talk to retentions"*.

If they try and backtrack you into the conversation again, simply stop, and ask again;

*'I'd like to talk to retentions please'*.

You should continue this until you are transferred to customer retentions. There is absolutely nothing wrong with repeating the same phrase over and over until you get the response you want.

Once you arrive with customer retentions, keep in mind what will happen here. They will be expecting you to leave, although they will be prepared to 'strike a deal' to keep you. You don't actually want to leave, but you would like a decent deal from them to stay.

If the conversation is awkward, and you seem to actually be heading down the cancellation route, restate what we've mentioned before.

Ask them what they will do to make you a happy customer again, explain simply what they have done wrong, use the 'Yes',

'No' questions to steer them into a position that puts them in the wrong, and in a position where something needs to be given to you to keep you.

A good real example here is with a digital TV provider; a fault with a cable/satellite box required a call to the company to get it fixed, they suggested an engineer come out to look at the box, and if needed, replace it with a refurbished box. The cost of this visit and replacement of  a once new box was about £60. They also gave an option of buying a brand new, higher spec box for about £120. A transfer to retentions took place, and the situation explained to them. During that explanation, it was explained that if this was the case, there was some considerable dissatisfaction with the company and we'd actually be thinking of leaving.

But how do we avoid actually leaving if we don't want to? The key here is being non committal about what you intend to do, whilst still inferring that you might leave;

*'I'm actually thinking of...'*

*'I might as well..' 'It seems sensible to..'*

This wording doesn't commit you to actually leaving, and it gives the conversation a route to be resolved. If you'd used the words;

*'I'm going to leave..'*

*'So disconnect me..'*

It's a lot more final, and committal, and really doesn't leave room for them, or you, to negotiate out of it.

In the case above the company in question started to shift their position slightly by offering to reduce the engineer fee. This is good, but, as we've mentioned previously 'if you don't like the answer, don't accept it'; putting a little more pressure on them, using the 'yes', 'no' questions, and what we have discussed previously, can help your position we can get more from them;

*'I've been with you for x years..'*

*'I've had repeated problems and issues..'*

*'I believe I can get a better deal with..'.*

In this situation, if the reduction of the engineer fee doesn't sound good, and it didn't in this case; you tell them that. Keep in mind you are the customer here, and they should be trying to keeping you.

The retort for this was;

'*so thats just letting me pay less for a refurbished box*'.

The final outcome was that retentions provided a deal by which a brand new, higher spec box, would be provided for £25. Which seemed much better than paying £60 for someone to come, declare a box dead and replace it with a low spec refurbished box.

In this case this was a good outcome, and accepted.

# CHAPTER FOURTEEN

## *Asking the Question*

At some during this whole process you will need to physically ask, or at least prompt the question of getting something back from the company in question.

There are two things to remember here… firstly, *When* do you ask the question, and secondly, *how* do you ask the question?

When do you ask? Well, quite simply; when you feel ready! That being said you should never 'ask the question' or hint at it until you have used everything we have talked about previously to establish that the company is at fault, and, more importantly that they company in question have, through the 'yes' and 'no' questions, and 'foot holes' dig themselves into a hole which the only way out of is by you asking 'the question'.

So how do you ask? There are a number of ways, and each will really depend on where you are in the food chain, and how the conversation is going.

One way is to just ask the following;

*"..and you'll be making some sort of gesture of good will?"*

A gesture of goodwill keeps it open as to what they will actually provide you with. You may find that you'll get a smallish amount possibly £10-£25.

Another way is to recap the time, and cost (calls etc) that you have spend talking to them;

*"This is now my 5th phone call to you… I repeatedly don't get an answer to my problem.."*

*"You seem unable to answer my question and resolve my*

*problem.. If you can't or won't, that fine, just tell me.."*

You can also tell them you've been told to speak to someone about a gesture of goodwill or remuneration or a some refund regarding your issue;

*"I've spoken to customer services who have advised me to talk to you about some sort of refund or gesture of goodwill to help resolve this.."*

In all cases you need to hint, or ask for *something*, but not be specific. Coming right out and saying that you'd like a specific amount refunded or given in a gesture will, normally not work. Like all good plans, if you convince them it's their idea, you'll have a much better result and success rate.

You will also sometimes get asked something like;

*"Well what do you want me to do, what do you want?"*

The first time I'm asked this question, I normally reply back with the 'naughty school child' type answer;

*"It's not for me to decide, you made the mistakes, you have broken the loyalty between us, and you need to think about what you have done, and what you can do to make me a happy customer again.."*

The second time I'm asked a similar question, I will probably then hint at what I actually want, remember what we decided at the beginning was going to be the outcome of our call? Why do I suggest something the second time round? The second time the company physically ask what I'd like, is confirmation that they themselves do not know what to provide me, and what I suggest cannot then be deemed a unreasonable request as I've given them the opportunity to offer something, and they haven't.

# CHAPTER FIFTEEN

## *Timeframes.*

You may get your desired outcome to your complaint there and then, but in most cases you won't. You will need to wait, be patient and await their response. But how long do you need to wait for an answer?

Sadly the simple answer to this is that 'it depends'; it both depends on the company, and the type of response you are looking for.

In the majority of cases if they are writing to you to confirm or resolve something, they have up to 14 days to just confirm your complaint. That is 14 days to just say, 'yes we know you have complained', they then have a further 60 days to resolve your complaint, but they can write to you to say they are still looking into the problem, and gain more time to respond.

In all my experience written communication from companies about complaints, isn't worth the paper its written on. They almost always boil down to a cut and paste type response that normally mentions the fact that 'your feedback has been noted', 'that unfortunately this is the standard procedure of the company', 'that they value customers', and will be signed by normally a person you've never heard of, or spoken to. You will also almost always get a free leaflet telling you how if you're not happy you can complain to a higher body (such as an ombudsman or similar).

My personal preference is to keep all the communication to verbal, either in person, or on the phone. It's a faster approach, and more dynamic, and flexible.

The important thing is to not let the company railroad you down the route of 'writing to you,' this will delay your case by a reasonable amount, and really end up without the answer you're looking for.

# CHAPTER SIXTEEN

## *Letters.*

Making a formal complaint, should be a simple task yes? Sadly not, pretty much every company still insist that you 'write to them' with your complaint. Some have caught up with technology, and allow you to 'email' them your complaint, but in all these cases, it still involves putting down the phone, writing something, and then putting the control of the complaint into their hands. You'll be waiting for a letter or email back from them and more importantly, they aren't dealing with you on the phone, and they have successfully herded you off into a pen, like a sheep being manoeuvred by a sheep dog.

The fact is that companies *have* to take formal complaints over the phone, they have the systems in front of them to record complaints and escalate them. However most, sadly, choose not to.

If they continue to push you towards writing to them with your complaint it is worth remembering that companies have a legal responsibility to take and handle complaints from customers. Continuing to push you towards writing to them, can, if you feel the need to, warrant a reminder to them of this fact, and again, give you another 'foot hole'.

Passing the buck of your complaint back to a complaints department address, which you will find oddly is populated by people who you cannot speak to on the phone, is as far as I'm concerned, a refusal to take a formal complaint.

You may need to go over this a few times with them, again

politely ask them to record the complaint, see what the reaction is, and again if you need to, repeat the reminder about their requirement to take a formal complaint, and their continued refusal to do so.

Even if they agree to take a formal complaint over the phone, their idea of the complaint and your's might be vastly different.

In many cases phone based complaints are treated as 'feedback'. Feedback doesn't need to be legally answered, its just filed somewhere. Check with them what they are going to do with your complaint and if it's going to be destined for the great feedback bin in the sky, or if they are actually going to deal with it. A good check here is to confirm the time frame for them formally responding to and confirming your complaint. It's normally 14 days for a written confirmation that at they least they acknowledge your complaint. If it sounds like theres no time frame to respond to your complaint, likelihood is that they will be treating this as 'feedback'.

Feedback is great, but it won't really solve or compensate you for your complaint. Once again, if your 'complaint' has been downgraded by them to 'feedback', remind them of the legal requirement for them to take a complaint, and so far, their refusal to do so;

"*I have now politely asked you to record and escalate a formal complaint, I have asked you to do this x times, and so far you have basically refused to do that, you are legally required to record and handle complaints and respond to them within the specified timeframes. I will ask you again to record my formal complaint..*"

If you have reached the point where you know they have formally recorded your complaint, well done, you have now laid the ground work to move on. Use everything we've discussed so far to move up the food chain, but with the fact that you're pushing yourself onwards with a formal complaint in your backpack..

If you do actually get a letter back from the company about your request, check that the letter isn't a 'cut and paste' letter.

A 'cut and paste' letter is basically a recycled letter, stating exactly the same information as a letter to another person that's complained, it's not committal, normally very uninformative, apologises generally, and states that really nothing more can be done. It sometimes wishes you well..

I call them cut and paste letters, because I did actually get one that still had the previous complainants name on it, and apologised for the issues I experienced in the Glasgow branch (I've never been to Glasgow in my life!). In fact the letter bore so little relevance to my complaint, it may as well have been from a completely different company. This is an extreme case, but, check the letters you get, do they actually talk about your issue, do they attempt to resolve it, or are they just 'cut and paste' letters.

If they are, if that letter is so worthless in your eyes at resolving your complaint, then its another 'foot hole' in the climb up the ladder.

Remember the person on the bottom of the letter that you've never heard of? No? Of course not, you've probably never spoken to them (they may not even exist)!. They are normally a facsimile signature of someone who has the job title of 'director of customer service' or similar.

My view is, and I think this should be yours as well, is that this person has sent you a letter, and signed it. Why not ring them and discuss the letter. You'll need to ring normally the main office, or customer services, and ask to talk to that person.

I'm slightly stubborn here, and I will attempt my hardest to get through to that person, you may not have the same success rate, assuming the person exists, and if they don't... thats a 'foot hole' (is it ok for a company to effectively lie about who signed a letter?)

Once through to that person, the one that 'signed' the letter, they may not actually know anything about the letter, its very unlikely that someone such as 'head of customer service' signs each and every letter going out. If they claim to not know about your issues, or the letter, state that their name is on the bottom of the letter, they, personally have signed your letter, they must have written it? No?

All you are doing here is really nullifying the letter, and proving that its basically a cut and paste response, and really, the case is still open, still unresolved, and they really haven't helped themselves by sending this letter out. At this point, you have another 'foot hole'

# CHAPTER SEVENTEEN
## *Vouchers.*

As a 'gesture of goodwill' you may often be offered 'coupons,' 'eVouchers' or similar. There is, or at least I think there is a big problem with this. The coupon or voucher will be of course to spend with the company in question, thus ensuring repeat business with them. They also in most cases really don't actually cost the company that amount of money. They are also normally fairly low in value, typically £5, £10 or similar, and of course, with anyone except the company that you are complaining to, worthless.

I believe that eVouchers and similar as a 'good will gesture' is a little insulting as well.. If you went to a theme park, and lets say suffered an injury on a ride, would you be pleased if you got a free pass to come again? Would you like to have a bad experience, and as a gesture of good will, a chance to come and have another one? Probably not. If your online shopping was delivered late repeatedly, would you like the chance to shop with them again with a voucher, and pay them more money, or would you like the choice to go elsewhere and spend your money? Certainly the second option gives you more freedom. But it is a personal choice, as to if you want a voucher, or, if you'd like some money back.

Because vouchers tend to be lower in value, if you decide to accept one, make sure you don't accept their first offer, but do keep in mind the value of your business on this occasion. A £5 voucher on a £10 purchase or service, is a reasonable outcome, and assuming you do wish to do business with them again, I'd actually accept that offer, if you don't wish to accept it a very simple;

*'A £5 voucher isn't actually acceptable'*

Will normally bat the problem back at them to solve.

In almost all circumstances they will normally double that almost straight away, but don't get into the 'no thats not enough' argument. If their next offer isn't good enough from your point of view, then its time to move up the food chain. Ask to talk to their manager, escalations, customer relations, or retentions, depending on where you currently are in the food chain.

# CHAPTER EIGHTEEN

## *How long have you spent?*

Your journey along your complaint might be a very long one, don't expect a 5 minute phone call. I say *your* journey might be a long one, this doesn't mean that who you're talking to has an equally long trip. You're likely to be transferred from one person to another, especially if you're moving up the food chain. When you arrive at your third member of staff, you may have spent 30 minutes on the phone, the third member of staff is going to be fresh as a daisy (at least to your complaint), it is always worth putting the amount of time you've spent on this conversation into the frame. This is especially true if you're asked to re-explain the nature of your call;

*'I have now spent 30 minutes on the phone, attempting to resolve a problem that really should, in all honesty be able to be resolved fairly quickly, and you are now asking me what the problem is?'*

Again use the fact that you have spoken to so many people, or spent so long on the phone as 'foot holes', use this to work your way up the food chain quicker.

# CHAPTER NINETEEN

## *Talking to the chief executive.*

The Chief Executive (or CEO) is basically about as high up as you can get. The CEO is Mr (or Mrs) Company, there is no-one higher than them and effectively the buck stops with them. In every single case when you complain to a company your trip up the food chain should done with the sole aim of talking to the CEO.

Unlikely as it seems or may sound, you can, with enough 'foot holes' and bluffing get to talk to them, or at the very least their personal assistant (or PA).

So how do you get to talk to this mythical person?

Well, there are multiple ways of getting there. One is once you feel you are high enough up the food chain, you need to request to talk to 'escalations'. This can jump you across the chasm of call centre staff and managers and into a blissful world where people believe your complaint is serious enough and badly managed enough to pay some major attention to it and try and resolve it. They also may just be sick of you at this point and want to pass you over! But regardless on their feelings at this point. It is a great place to head to. It is from here that you can then request that the matter be raised with the Executive Office.

Another route, and this is a leap of faith and a bit cheeky, is to go direct to the Executive Office of the company. You must have your wits about you for this, and be willing to bluff you way in. During this process you must be totally confident in your abilities to go straight to the CEO office.

So how do we get there?

You'll need to make two calls. You're first will be to the normal call centre staff. Go through as much of the process that I've previously written about as you can, until you feel like you have either hit a brick wall, or you just wish to jump direct to the CEO level.

When talking with the customer service person, you need to simply state that you will be ringing the CEO after this call. You may get a number of different responses to this, but what you are basically looking for here is agreement from them that you can do it. You're not seeking permission, you'll see why in a moment.

I find something simple such as;

*"Once I've finished this call, my next call will be to your CEO"*

Works just fine.

You need a response such as;

*"That fine, if you wish to do that"*

*"That is up to you if you want to do that"*

*"You're entitled to do that if you want"*

..or something similar. Once you're fairly happy that the customer service person has acknowledged that you're going to ring the CEO, and that they are not telling you not to, say goodbye, and then move onto the next bit.

You will now need to ring through the company switch board. You can just ask a customer service person on the phone for the head office number. They should know it (and if they don't, this is another 'foot hole'), or just google the company name and 'head office' to get some leads. You'll often find the head office telephone number on 'investor relations' pages, or sometimes against various things like job listings, shareholder reports and such.

You will get through to normally the main switchboard at the head office. The route to the CEO office will vary, but the following has worked for me;

Ask politely to talk to the executive office, if they query this, politely respond that you want to talk to Mr Smith's office, the chief executive. They will normally ask your name, and sometimes what it is regarding. You may also get asked if the CEO's office is expecting your call. I have normally then said that they are expecting my call. This hasn't been a lie, because as we've just mentioned above, we've told the previous call centre staff that my next call is the Executive Office, and they agreed I could do that. So you can, with complete honesty say that they CEO is expecting your call.

If you are totally lucky here, the receptionist will pass you through to the executive office, you'll normally get through to a personal assistant (who's aim here is to make sure that the CEO isn't disturbed), or, you may need to do some more persuading of the switchboard operator to pop you through. Keep confident, and polite here, explain that you have been advised that you can talk to the CEO (from our previous call centre conversation), and that you'd like to talk to them. Keep at it, keep repeating the same responses, and hold any refusals as 'foot holes' when you finally do get through.

If you are asked if you have spoken to the executive office before, the answer is a very confident "yes," if you are asked what it is about, don't explain, as they will pass you straight into customer services. The answer there is something similar to;

*"It's an ongoing issue and I've been advised that I need to talk to the executive office"*

Once you are with the CEO office, you'll likely be talking to a member of the executive office staff, possibly a personal assistant, someone in the executive escalations team or similar. Have no doubt, it is very unlikely that you will be talking to the CEO. But once you do get through, well done, you will have reached basically the peak of Everest so to speak. Once you have access to the Executive office, all manner of magical things can be achieved.

Whomever you are now talking to, you need to get their name, and switch on some charm and get them on your side as soon as possible. A sigh, and a *"I really hope you can restore my faith in your company, I've been trying to talk to someone who can help and resolve my issue"*

..or similar sometime set you on the right foot.

Once you are on the right foot with these people, you can, within reason pretty much just ask them for what you want. At this level they have the power to work miracles. I've had bills zero'ed, large credits applied to my account, installations done free, replacement equipment, upgrades, loyalty discounts applied, and in one case, I even had a card, flowers and bottle of wine from the CEO office!

But whatever the case, you will get two things, something to make you a happy customer again, and more importantly, some form of repentance from the company itself

# CHAPTER TWENTY
## *Effective Complaining*

There are many things that we've covered in this book, and to effectively 'complain' and get something more than sorry back, you'll need to understand all the things I've written about, and use them as and when you need them during your conversation with the company in question.

It's worth going through and summarise the key points.

- Work out before you start, roughly what you are trying to do, and what do you actually want.
- Make sure that it doesn't cost you money to complain.
- Make sure that whatever conversation you have, you don't make it personal with the person you are talking to. Make it about the 'company'
- Make sure that when you talk to the company, you sit, or stand, depending on how you need to come across.
- You can ask for a 'gesture of good will' at any point to receive back something to make you feel better..
- You need to work up the "food chain", moving up towards, hopefully the Chief Executive (or CEO). Do this by asking to talk to a manager each time you feel you are getting stuck.
- Don't be rude, be polite and be factual, you can bluff, but don't lie about anything.
- Don't accept wishy washy answers, like 'maybe', 'probably', and 'possibly'.

- Use 'foot holes', that is things the company continue to do wrongly to move up the food chain, and use the right language.
- Establish 'Yes' or 'No' answers to questions to set key facts.
- Demonstrate to them the pain you have gone through, again with 'Yes' or 'No' answers.
- Don't forget for an easy win, most first line operators can provide 'gestures of goodwill' up to £25.
- Whoever you talk to, make sure they give you their Call Centre or Operator ID.
- Make sure that the person you talk to 'Knows their own business', they shouldn't be replying with 'I don't know', 'I've spoken to.. And they say..'
- Don't accept 'call backs' unless you are at a very high level (like escalation's or the CEO office).
- Remember that if you don't like the the answer, don't accept it!
- There are many ways that you can get the attention of a company, and make them see you point of view by making them think about what they have done.
- You can give them the choice of you leaving and going to another supplier.
- Choose when to ask 'The question' of getting something back from them, ask at the right time, and in the right way
- You don't have to write to a company to complain, but if you feel the need to, make sure they don't just fob you off with standard letters.
- Decide if you want to accept eVouchers or coupons as 'gestures of goodwill' if they are offered.
- Make sure they continually know how long you have wasted talking to them.
- Always aim to get up the food chain to the Chief Executive. You can do it..

If you follow the ideas and processes in this little book, you should find that complaining to a company will result in something a little more than just 'sorry'. Have faith in what you are talking to them about, stick to your guns, and don't give up..

I wish you luck…

19363062R00035

Printed in Great Britain
by Amazon